MAD

THE HALF-WIT AND WISDOM OF ALFRED E. NEUMAN

CLASSIC PEARLS OF IDIOCY · ILLUSTRATED BY SERGIO ARAGONÉS

WARNER ✺ TREASURES®

PUBLISHED BY WARNER BOOKS

A TIME WARNER COMPANY

Though Alfred E. Neuman wasn't the first to say
"A fool and his money are soon parted," here's your chance
to prove the old adage right—subscribe to *MAD!* Simply
call 1-800-4-MADMAG and mention code 5BKA7.
Operators are standing by (the water cooler).

Warner Treasures name and logo
are registered trademarks of
Warner Books, Inc.
1271 Avenue of the Americas
New York, NY 10020

Visit our Web site at http://pathfinder.com/twep
Visit MAD Online through AOL. Call 1-800-203-2600.

A Time Warner Company
Printed in Singapore

First Printing: March 1997
10 9 8 7 6 5 4 3 2 1
ISBN: 0-446-91200-X

Book design by Flag

In memory of
the countless jokes
that have died on the pages of *MAD*
magazine, and the readers who
mourn their loss!

With a special tip of the
MAD dunce cap to Lucille Goodyear,
Jerry DeFuccio, and Jeff Rovin, not
to mention Grant Geissman.

CONTENTS

WORDS TO LIVE BY

It's a good idea to keep your
you never know when

words soft and sweet because
you'll have to eat them.

Live every day as if it were your last, because one of these days you'll be right!

It's what you learn after you know it all that really counts.

You'll never get rid of a bad temper by losing it!

If at first you don't

succeed . . . you're about normal.

Experience is something you never have until just after you need it.

Life is what happens to you while you're busy making future plans.

When you're in deep water,
it's a good idea to keep your
mouth shut!

These days, the only time politicians are telling the truth is when they call each other a liar.

It's no wonder politicians don't listen to their conscience.
They don't want to take advice from a total stranger.

The reason politicians are so busy is that they spend half their time passing laws and the other half helping their friends get around them.

The ups and downs of
the economy are the
result of having elected
too many yo-yos!

Isn't it amazing how political candidates can give you all their good points and qualifications in a thirty-second TV commercial?

Elections are when people find out what politicians stand for and politicians find out what people will fall for.

Political campaign speeches are like steer horns: a point here, a point there ... and a lot of bull in between!

Have you noticed that
political promises are
usually in one year and out
the other?

It's astonishing how politicians never say anything, yet always insist they're being misquoted.

America is the land that fought for freedom and then began passing laws to get rid of it.

War is what happens when arms are used instead of heads!

Too many politicians who wave the flag want to waive what it stands for.

Ever notice how many government officials make their raises effective long before *they* ever are?

Remember the good old days, when the government lived within its income and without most of yours?

Ever notice that to entertain some people all you have to do is listen?

Some minds are like concrete . . . all mixed up and permanently set.

It's not just the ups and downs that make life difficult, it's the jerks.

The reason most people are lost in thought is because it's unfamiliar territory.

If most people said what's on their minds, they'd be speechless.

How is it that people looking for a helping hand tend to overlook the one at the end of their arm?

You never know how many friends you have until you own a summer place!

Vision is what some people claim they have when they find that they've guessed correctly.

Most of us don't know exactly what we want, but we're pretty sure we don't have it.

An argument is two
people trying to get the last
word in first!

There was a time when a preacher's Little Black Book was a Bible!

When most people put in their two cents' worth, they are not overcharging.

Ever notice how people who say, "That's the way the ball bounces" are usually the ones who dropped it?

People with bad

coughs should go to doctors
instead of theaters.

Even the man who has everything is envious of the man who has two of everything.

Germs attack people where they're
weakest—which is why there are
so many head colds.

A masochist is one
who paints himself into a corner
and then applies a second coat.

Too often, people
who want to offer sound
advice give us more sound
than advice.

Good hospitality is making your guests feel at home, even when you wish they were!

Modesty is the art of drawing attention to whatever it is you're being humble about.

Most people don't act stupid— it's the real thing!

When you give back all your ill-gotten gains, you're a reformed crook. When you keep most of the loot and only give back a small part of it, you're a philanthropist.

It's called take-home pay because there's nowhere else you can go with it!

Misers are tough to live with, but they make terrific ancestors!

Living on a budget is the same as living beyond your means, except that now you have a record of it.

Most people get into financial difficulty when they don't act their wage.

Today, money still talks. Trouble is, you have to increase the volume a lot!

Ever notice how random chance always picks you for jury duty, but never to win the lottery?

The dollar will never fall as

will do

low as what some people

to get it!

When money talks, nobody
criticizes its accent!

Why is it that things always look greener in the other guy's wallet?

Your money and
your vacation never seem
to run out at the
same time.

Sometimes, the best scheme for doubling your money is to fold it in half and stuff it back in your wallet.

These days, most people's bank accounts need month-to-month resuscitation!

Astronomers point out
away from the Earth at
Can you

that the universe is racing

15,000 miles per second.

blame it?

Today's "non-conformists" are getting harder and harder to tell apart.

The trouble with modern apartments
is: the walls are too thin when
you try to sleep, and too thick when
you try to listen.

Blessed are the censors, for they shall inhibit the Earth.

A supermarket is where you spend half an hour hunting for instant coffee!

You know the world's in trouble when it takes 2,000 laws just to enforce the Ten Commandments!

The suburbs are where they cut down all the trees and then name the streets after them.

Only in America could a
letter that offers a prize of ten million
dollars be regarded as junk mail.

Nuclear energy may be one thing
that will finally prove to us that all
men are cremated equal.

The great advantage of compact cars is that you can get twice as many of them into traffic jams.

The trouble with most neighborhoods is that there are too many hoods in them, and not enough neighbors.

We're living in an age
when lemonade is made with
artificial ingredients and
furniture polish is made
with real lemons.

A man will go out with a woman if she's really different from other women . . . the difference being she'll go out with him.

Notice how women who claim that all men are alike seldom have trouble spotting the difference between you and Tom Cruise?

The first thing a
man notices about a
woman . . . depends
on which way
she's going!

A wedding ring is like a tourniquet—it cuts off your circulation!

A kiss is valid
proof that two heads are
better than one.

Some people are like blisters: they show up right after the work is done.

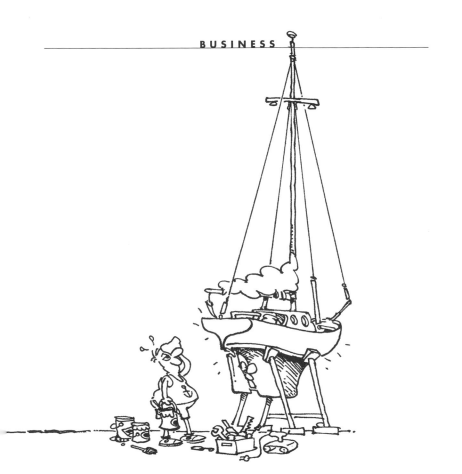

The big guns in business are those who haven't as yet been fired!

Most people are too lazy to open the door when opportunity knocks.

Before arguing with your boss, it may be well to look at both sides: their side . . . and the outside.

A born executive is someone whose father owns the business.

An employer is someone who's late
when you're early and early when
you're late.

A successful person is a clod like you
who worked harder.

A lawyer is someone who writes an eighty-page document and calls it a brief.

The early bird gets the worm . . . but look what happens to the early worm!

The Half-Wit and Wisdom of Alfred E. Neuman

The problem with the ladder of success is that by the time you've climbed it, you're considered over the hill!

It's really amazing how unimportant your job is when you ask for a raise . . . and how important it is when you want a day off!

As you get older, work seems a lot less fun, and fun seems a lot more work!

Raising children is like taking pictures: you never know how they'll come out!

Marriage is like drugs to some people: they keep taking one kind of dope after another.

A family vacation is when
you go away with people
you need to get away from.

Adam was lucky! He never had to
listen to Eve talk about the other men
she could have married.

Adolescence is that period in a
child's life when parents become
most difficult!

Marriage is like a bath:
once you're into it and you're used
to it, it's not so hot.

What—me worry?